SNAKES

Design   David West
                  Children's Book Design
Designer   Flick Killerby
Editor   Charles DeVere
Picture Researcher Emma Krikler
Illustrator   Adrian Lascom

© Aladdin Books 1992

First published in
the United States in 1992 by
Gloucester Press Inc
95 Madison Avenue
New York, NY 10016

Library of Congress Cataloging-in-Publication Data

Robson, Denny.
    Snakes / by Denny Robson.
        p.   cm. — (Let's look up)
    Includes index.
    Summary: Explores the different characteristics of snakes.
    ISBN 0-531-17355-0
    1. Snakes—Juvenile literature. (1. Snakes.) I. Title.
    QL666.06R49   1992
    597.96—dc20   91-34967   CIP   AC

Printed in Belgium

LET'S LOOK UP

SNAKES

DENNY ROBSON

GLOUCESTER PRESS
New York : London : Toronto : Sydney

Contents

Fangs and poison	6
The big squeeze	8
Snake senses	10
Food and feasting	12
Protection	14
Snake enemies	17
Snake babies	18
Growing	20
In the trees	22
In the water	24
Snakes worldwide	26
Moving snakefacts	28
Amazing snakes	30
Glossary and index	32

About this book
You can decide for yourself how to read this book. You can simply read it straight through, or you can follow the arrows to find out more about a subject before you go on. The choice is yours!

Follow the arrows if you want to know more....

Introduction

Many people think that snakes are slimy, dangerous creatures. But their scaly skins are dry and cool, and only a very few snakes are harmful to humans. Most snakes live in the warmer parts of the world, in deserts, tropical forests, and grasslands. Some spend their lives on the ground, others in trees, and some in rivers and seas. Snakes come in a wide range of sizes and colors, and live their lives in very many different ways.

Most snakes are shy, but it's best to take care when walking where they live.

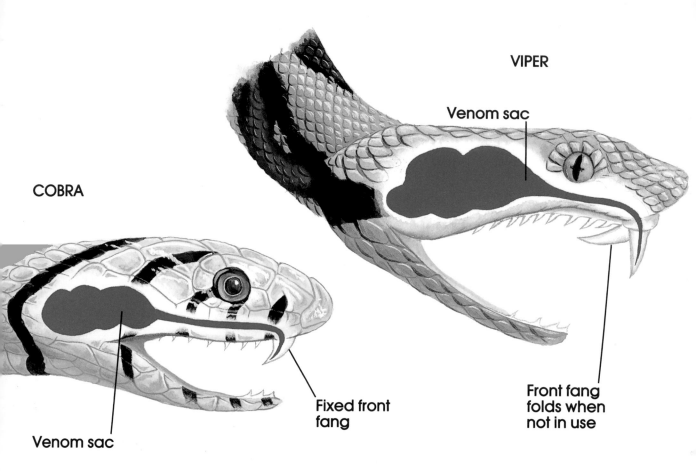

VIPER

Venom sac

COBRA

Fixed front fang

Front fang folds when not in use

Venom sac

Fangs and poison

Only about one third of all snakes are poisonous. These snakes use poison, or venom, to catch food and defend themselves from their enemies. The poison also makes it easier for them to digest their prey. The snake's forked tongue is not poisonous, as some people think. Poison is kept in sacs inside the mouth. When the snake strikes, it runs from the sacs into the snake's fangs.

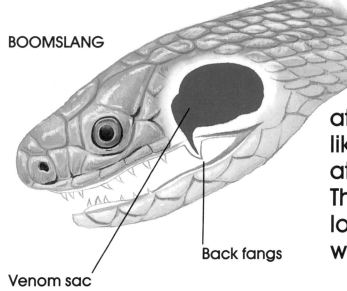

BOOMSLANG

Venom sac

Back fangs

Poisonous snakes may have fangs at the back of their mouths, like the boomslang, or fixed at the front, like the cobra. The viper's fangs are so long that they fold back when the mouth is closed.

Which is the most poisonous snake of all?

The king cobra is the biggest poisonous snake, growing up to 18 feet long. Its bite could kill a human in a few minutes. But the most poisonous snake of all is a sea snake of N.W. Australian waters. Its poison is a hundred times stronger than any other snake's.

A sea snake's venom is deadly.

If you want to know more about poisonous snakes, turn to Snakes worldwide

PAGE 26

The big squeeze

Constrictors are snakes that coil themselves around their victims and squeeze, or constrict, until their prey stops breathing. Pythons and boas are constricting snakes. They include some of the biggest reptiles in the world. They are often strong and skillful hunters. Most of the animals they catch are quite small, but large pythons can kill antelope and deer.

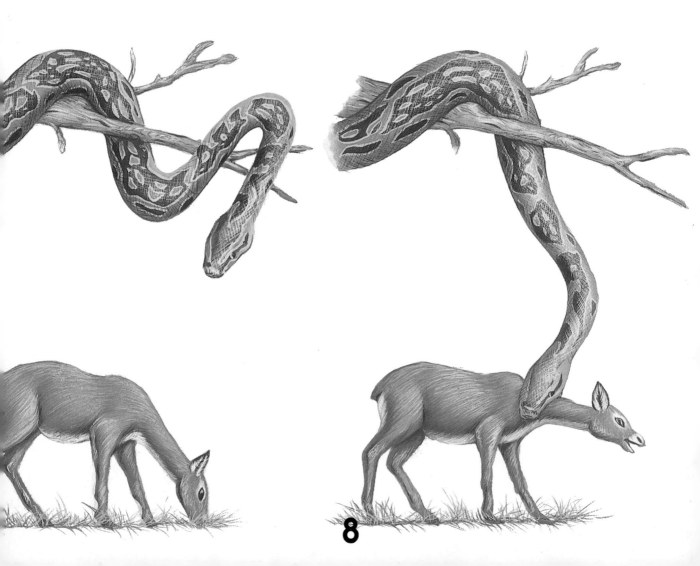

Which is the biggest snake in the world?

▷ A reticulated python

The heaviest snakes are the South American anacondas. But the longest snake recorded was a reticulated python in the Philippines – 33 feet long!

If you want to know which is the smallest snake in the world, turn to Amazing snakes

PAGE 30

A rock python lies in wait and then strikes and suffocates a small deer.

Snakes have no ears, but they can feel vibrations in the ground. They also have well developed eyesight. A snake's flickering tongue is a very important part of its senses. It tests the air and ground for scents given off by other animals, and places these scents in a special organ in the roof of the mouth, called Jacobson's organ. The snake can then follow the scent trail of its prey.

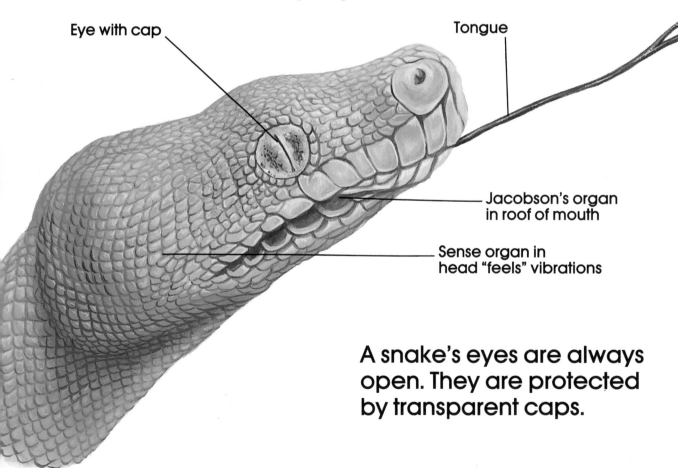

Eye with cap

Tongue

Jacobson's organ in roof of mouth

Sense organ in head "feels" vibrations

A snake's eyes are always open. They are protected by transparent caps.

Do all snakes have the same senses?

A pit viper or a rattlesnake, which belong to the same family, has an extra sense. It has two hollows, or pits, on its face. The pits can feel the body heat of the prey so that the snake can hunt even in the dark.

This is a pit viper. Can you see the pit on the side of its face?

If you want to know more about rattlesnakes, turn to Growing

PAGE 20

Food and feasting

A snake swallows its victim whole, even when the victim is much, much wider than the snake's head! It can do this because of its amazing jaws. They move apart so that the mouth opens very wide. The snake's skin stretches as it swallows its prey. Snakes don't need to burn up food to keep warm and so they don't have to eat often. A python might go for a year between meals!

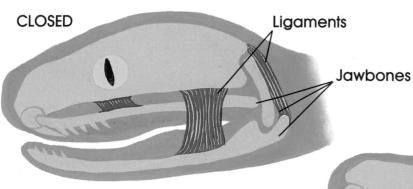

CLOSED

Ligaments

Jawbones

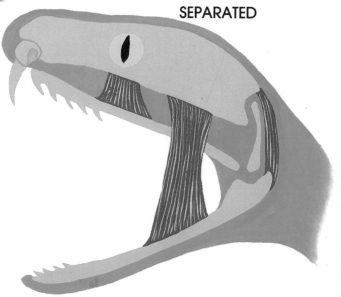

SEPARATED

The two halves of a snake's jaw are joined only by ligaments. The jaws can move far apart, down, and outward.

How do pythons swallow large prey?

The python has backward pointing teeth that pull prey into its mouth. The jaws then "walk" forward over the prey. A snake has no hip or shoulder bones to get in the way when it swallows prey.

If you want to know more about snake skeletons, turn to Moving snakefacts

PAGE 28

This is an egg-eating snake. When the snake has eaten the egg, it will spit out the shell.

Protection

Many snakes are protected by their coloring. Some are camouflaged to blend in with their surroundings. Tree pythons, for example, are green like leaves. Other snakes have stripes or blotches that break up their outlines and make them difficult to see. If snakes are threatened, they defend themselves in a number of different ways.

Ball python
The ball python rolls itself into a ball for protection.

BALL
PYTHON

SPITTING
COBRA

SIDEWINDER

Sidewinder
The sidewinder buries itself in the sand to protect itself from its enemies and the hot sun.

Why are some snakes boldly marked?

Coral snakes are very poisonous. Their bright red, yellow, and black bands are a warning signal to other animals to keep away. Other harmless snakes, like milk snakes, mimic these colors to fool an enemy into thinking that they, too, are dangerous.

Dangerous coral snake

Harmless milk snake

If you want to know more about snake defenses, turn to Amazing snakes

PAGE 30

Spitting cobra
The spitting cobra squirts a stream of poison at its enemy's face, often blinding it.

This hawk is feeding on a snake. Other birds of prey, such as eagles, owls and secretary birds all kill and eat snakes.

snake enemies

There are lots of animals that see snakes as a tasty meal. Birds of prey hunt snakes and big cats will attack even the largest pythons. Snakes are not even safe from their own kind. The king snake feeds on other snakes, even poisonous rattlesnakes! But the biggest threat of all comes from humans. People kill millions of snakes every year.

Why do people kill snakes?

People kill snakes out of fear, for food and for their skins, which can be sold for a lot of money. Millions of others die when the places in which they live are destroyed, like the rainforests.

Snakeskin leather goods

If you want to know more about where different snakes come from, turn to Snakes worldwide

PAGE 26

Snake babies

Like most reptiles, snakes lay eggs. Pythons curl around their eggs to keep them warm, while others lay them in warm "nests" of rotting plants. The young snake breaks through the leathery shell of its egg with a special "egg tooth." Some snakes keep their eggs inside their bodies and then lay small living snakes. Young poisonous snakes can bite the moment they are hatched!

How quickly do young snakes grow?

Baby snakes are able to take care of themselves right away. They can grow quickly. A python may be up to two feet on hatching and over six feet long a year later.

Yellow anaconda and young

If you want to know more about how snakes grow, turn to Growing

PAGE 20

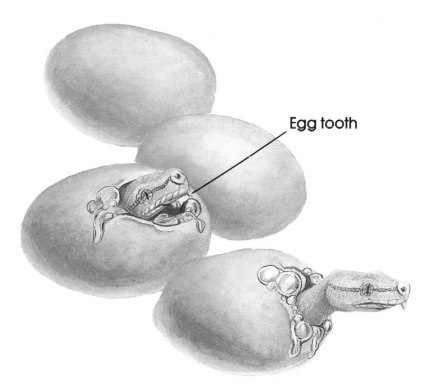

Egg tooth

The young snake cuts a hole in the shell with its sharp egg tooth. The tooth is lost soon after the snake wriggles out.

19

Growing

Snakes keep growing, even when they are adult. But a snake's skin does not grow with it, so in order to get bigger, the snake must shed its skin. This happens several times a year. When the skin becomes worn, it splits and the snake wriggles out, head first. The snake has a new skin under the old one which looks as if it has been newly painted.

△ A diamondback rattlesnake, the most dangerous in America, sheds its skin.

How long do snakes live?

Snakes can live for up to 40 years. The snakes that live longest are probably the biggest snakes, the constrictors.

Anaconda

If you want to know more about different constrictors, turn to Snakes worldwide

PAGE 26

The deadly rattlesnake shakes the rattle at the end of its tail when alarmed. The rattle is made of loosely-linked rings. A new ring is added each time the snake sheds its skin.

In the trees

Many snakes live in trees. The emerald tree boa from South America, for example, is perfectly suited to life in the trees. Its beautiful green coloring and white markings make it hard to spot against the leafy background. It hunts lizards and birds which it seizes with its long front teeth. Some tree snakes can actually glide from tree to tree.

How do snakes climb trees?

This is a golden tree snake. To climb, the snake grips the rough tree bark with its large belly scales and then thrusts itself forward. Its strong tail helps it anchor itself to the branches.

If you want to know more about how snakes move, turn to Moving snakefacts

PAGE 28

△ A green tree snake from East Africa

Malayan golden
tree snake

"Flying snakes"

When the snake launches itself from a branch, it spreads its ribs and flattens its belly to make a curved surface. This traps air, like a parachute. The snake holds its body in an "S" shape and uses its tail to steer.

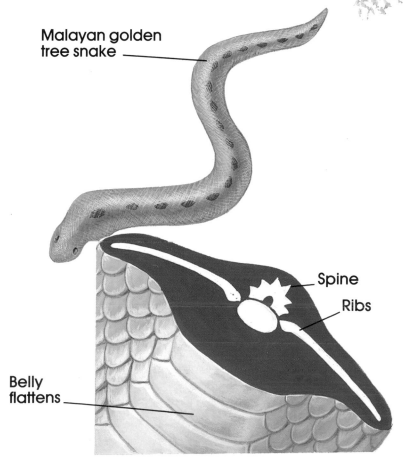

Spine

Ribs

Belly
flattens

23

In the water

The South American anacondas are huge snakes that spend their days in or near rivers or lakes. They hunt at dusk, seizing small mammals as they come to drink, or they swim through the water searching for prey.

Most sea snakes live in the Indian and Pacific oceans. They kill fish with a powerful poison. Their flattened tails help them to swim and they can cover their nostrils when they dive.

Anacondas are fast, strong swimmers. They are constricting snakes. They will either suffocate their prey or drown it before eating it.

▽ An anaconda searches the river for fish or even caiman.

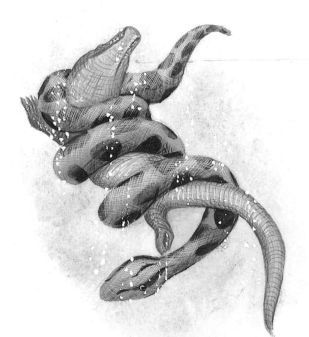

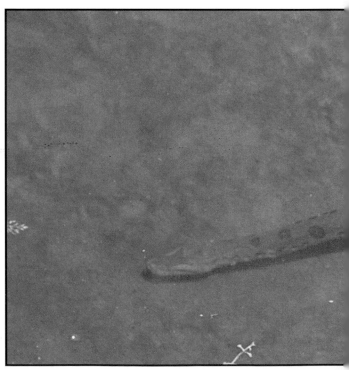

Do sea snakes spend all their lives in the sea?

Some sea snakes live along the shore and only go into the sea to catch food. Others never go ashore at all, feeding, breeding, and dying in the sea. There are about fifty species of sea snakes.

If you want to know more about the different species of snake, turn to Snakes worldwide

PAGE 26

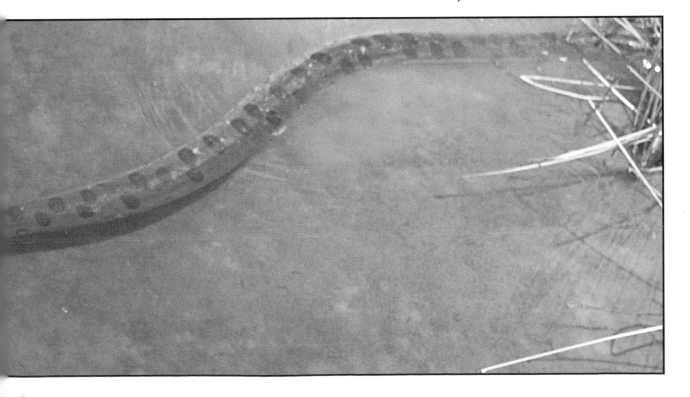

Snakes worldwide

There are around 2,700 different species of snake. This chart shows some of them and gives you an idea of their size. The side of each square represents 6 in. p = poisonous c = constrictor

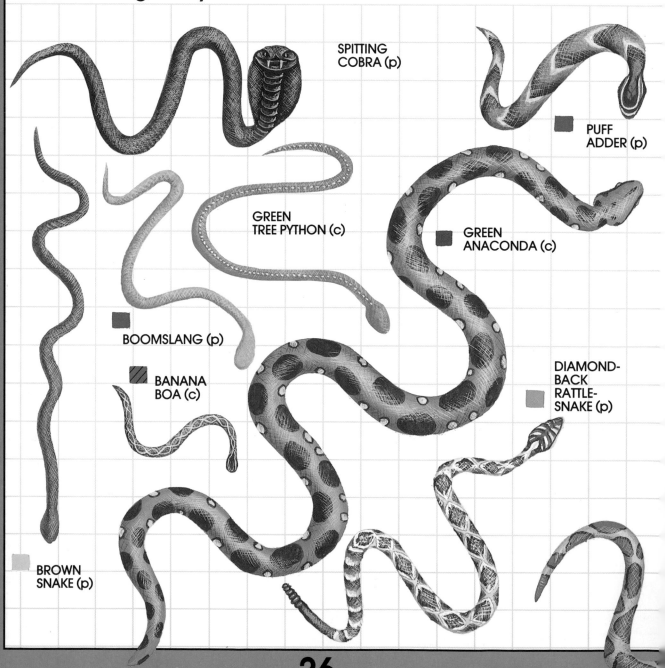

SPITTING COBRA (p)

PUFF ADDER (p)

GREEN TREE PYTHON (c)

GREEN ANACONDA (c)

BOOMSLANG (p)

BANANA BOA (c)

DIAMOND-BACK RATTLE-SNAKE (p)

BROWN SNAKE (p)

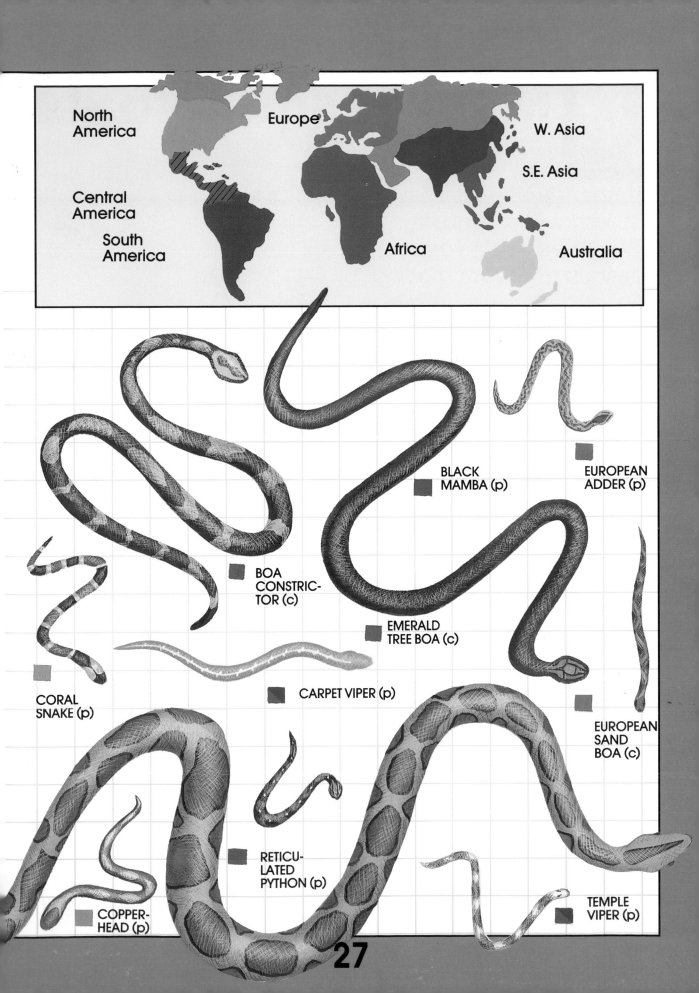

North America

Europe

W. Asia

S.E. Asia

Central America

South America

Africa

Australia

BLACK MAMBA (p)

EUROPEAN ADDER (p)

BOA CONSTRIC-TOR (c)

EMERALD TREE BOA (c)

CORAL SNAKE (p)

CARPET VIPER (p)

EUROPEAN SAND BOA (c)

RETICU-LATED PYTHON (p)

COPPER-HEAD (p)

TEMPLE VIPER (p)

27

Moving snakefacts

As snakes have no legs, they have had to develop their own ways of moving on land. They move by pushing against the surface that they are resting on.

Tail

Backbones

Ribs

Serpentine
Most snakes move like this, curving their bodies and pushing against rocks and bumps on the surface of the ground.

The inside story
To be able to bend in so many directions, snakes have to have very strong and flexible skeletons. They have very long backbones and hundreds of ribs.

Straight line

Heavy snakes like pythons and boas creep slowly in a straight line. They use the scales on their bellies to dig into the ground and pull themselves along.

Concertina

Using its tail as a lever, the snake thrusts its head and neck forward. Then it presses its neck to the ground and pulls the rest of its body along.

Sidewinder

A sidewinder arches its head to the side, then draws up its body to join it. This keeps much of its body off the hot desert sand.

Skull

Amazing snakes

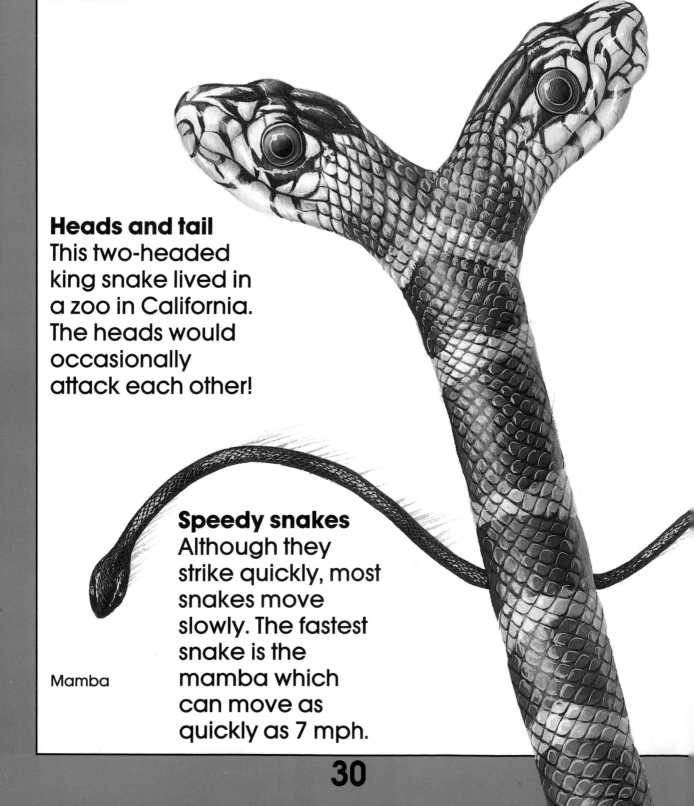

Heads and tail
This two-headed king snake lived in a zoo in California. The heads would occasionally attack each other!

Mamba

Speedy snakes
Although they strike quickly, most snakes move slowly. The fastest snake is the mamba which can move as quickly as 7 mph.

A grass snake "playing dead"

Rubber boa

Great Pretenders

When a hognosed snake or a grass snake is threatened, it pretends to be dead so that its enemy will leave it alone! It rolls over and "plays dead" with its mouth open and tongue hanging out.

When the rubber boa is threatened, it coils itself into a ball. It hides its head, and instead waves its tail at its enemy, pretending the tail is its head. If the enemy attacks, only the tail is damaged and so the snake survives.

Tiny snakes

The world's smallest snake is the thread snake of the West Indies. It is only about half an inch long and so thin that if you took the lead out of your pencil, it could wriggle through the hole!

Thread snake

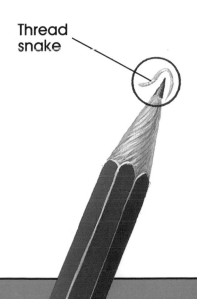

Glossary

Camouflage The color and shape of animals which allows them to blend in with their background and not be seen by their enemies.

Cold-blooded Reptiles are cold-blooded – they cannot control their body temperature. They warm up and cool down with their surroundings.

Constrictor A snake which wraps its body around its prey and squeezes until the prey has suffocated.

Prey Animals that are hunted by other animals for food.

Species Animals and plants that have the same structure and can reproduce together.

Venomous snakes Snakes which kill using poison.

Index

anaconda 9, 21, 24, 26

boomslang 7, 26

camouflage 14
constrictor snakes 8
coral snake 15, 26

eggs 18

fangs 6
food 12
"flying snakes" 23

hatching 18, 19

Jacobson's organ 10

nests 18

poison 6
poison sacs 6
pythons 8, 12, 13, 19, 26, 27

rattlesnakes 11, 20, 21, 26

sidewinder 14, 29
snake jaws 12

PHOTOCREDITS
All pictures in the book are supplied by Bruce Coleman Limited apart from page 21 which is from Partridge Productions/Oxford Scientific Films.

PRINTED IN BELGIUM BY
proost
INTERNATIONAL BOOK PRODUCTION